SPUNKY
SCIENCE

SPUNKY SCIENCE

CAN

- Make copies for your students for admin use

- Print them in different fonts such as a booklet

- Print in various sizes to fit your needs

- Post content on a school-based platform for student use or reference

CAN'T

- Distribute digital or copies to others without an additional purchase

- Remove Spunky Science logo or copyright

- Resell or redistribute in any way other than originally intended by Spunky Science

TABLE OF CONTENTS

SPUNKY SCIENCE

FROM MOLECULES TO ORGANISMS

FROM
MOLECULES TO
ORGANISMS

CELLS

Unicellular

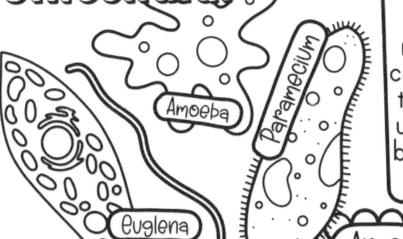

Amoeba

Paramecium

Euglena

All living things are made up of cells, which is the smallest unit that can be said to be alive.

An organism may consist of one single cell

Or many different numbers and types of cells.

Multicellular

Spunky Science ™

CELL STRUCTURES

Within cells, special structures are responsible for particular functions.

The **CELL MEMBRANE** forms a boundary that controls what enters and leaves the cell.

MITOCHONDRIA produce the energy necessary for the cell's survival and functioning.

The **NUCLEUS** is the largest organelle inside the cell. The functions of the nucleus are that it houses its DNA.

CHLOROPLASTS produce energy through photosynthesis and oxygen-release processes

CELL WALL provides structural strength and support, and also provide a semi-permeable surface for molecules to pass in and out of the cell.

Spunky Science ™

CELLULAR SYSTEMS

In multicellular systems bodies are a system of multiple interacting subsystems. The systems are groups of cells that work together to form tissues and organs that are specialized for particular body functions.

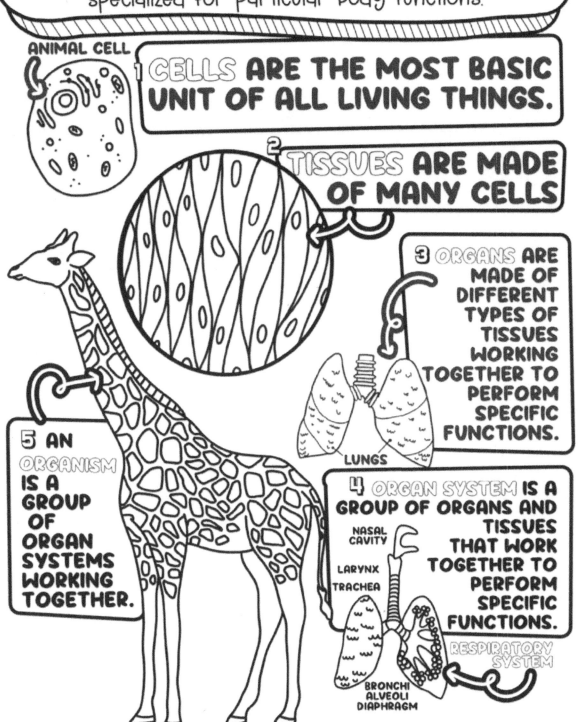

ANIMAL CELL

1 CELLS ARE THE MOST BASIC UNIT OF ALL LIVING THINGS.

2 TISSUES ARE MADE OF MANY CELLS

3 ORGANS ARE MADE OF DIFFERENT TYPES OF TISSUES WORKING TOGETHER TO PERFORM SPECIFIC FUNCTIONS.

LUNGS

5 AN ORGANISM IS A GROUP OF ORGAN SYSTEMS WORKING TOGETHER.

4 ORGAN SYSTEM IS A GROUP OF ORGANS AND TISSUES THAT WORK TOGETHER TO PERFORM SPECIFIC FUNCTIONS.

NASAL CAVITY

LARYNX

TRACHEA

RESPIRATORY SYSTEM

BRONCHI
ALVEOLI
DIAPHRAGM

Spunky Science ™

4 TYPES OF TISSUES
IN THE HUMAN BODY

CONNECTIVE

Tissue that connects, supports, binds, or separates other tissues or organs.

EPITHELIAL

Tissue that forms the covering on all internal and external organs. They serve as a protective barrier as well as secreting and absorbing substances.

MUSCLE

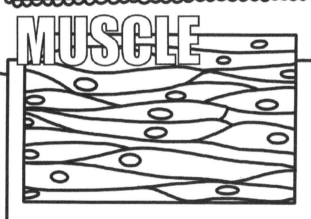

Tissue that attach to bones or internal organs and blood vessels and are responsible for movement.

NERVOUS

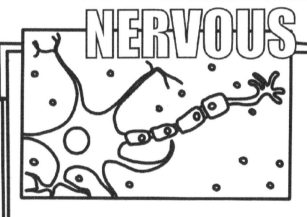

Tissues that are the main component of the nervous system-made of primarily neurons and glial cells.

Spunky Science ™

ANIMAL SURVIVAL

Animals engage in characteristic behaviors that increase the odds of reproduction.

Vocalization of animals & colorful plumage to attract mates for breeding.

Nest building to protect young from cold

BiRD OF PARADiSE

Herding of animals to protect young from predators

Spunky Science ™

PLANT SURVIVAL

Plants reproduce in a variety of ways sometimes depending on animal behavior and specialized features for reproduction.

Bright flowers attracting butterflies that transfer pollen

Flower nectar and odors that attract insects that transfer pollen

This squirrel will bury this nut which will eventually grow into a tree

Spunky Science ™

GENETIC FACTORS

Genetic factors affect the growth of the adult plant.

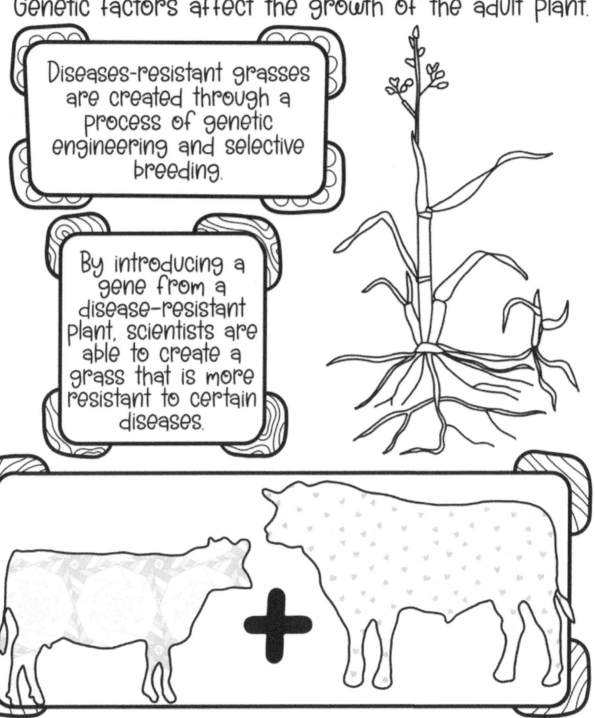

Diseases-resistant grasses are created through a process of genetic engineering and selective breeding.

By introducing a gene from a disease-resistant plant, scientists are able to create a grass that is more resistant to certain diseases.

Farmers selectively breed different types of cows with highly desirable characteristics in order to produce the best meat and dairy.

LOCAL FACTORS

Local environmental conditions could affect species growth and development. These conditions include availability of food, light, space, and water.

DROUGHT

Decreasing Plant Growth

FERTILIZER

Increasing plant growth

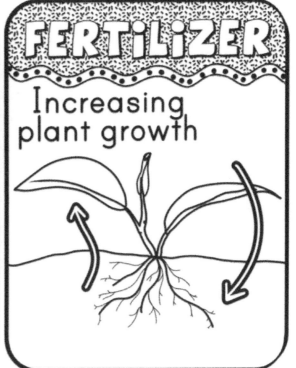

SEED VARIETY

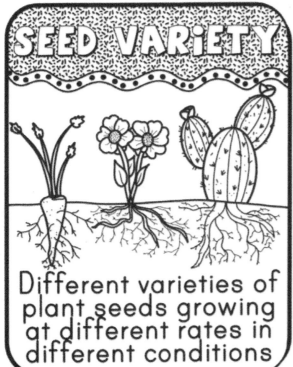

Different varieties of plant seeds growing at different rates in different conditions

POND SIZE

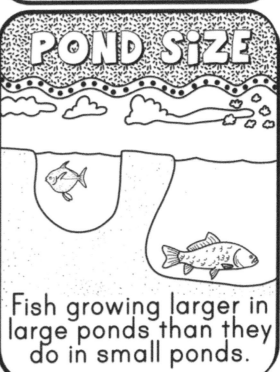

Fish growing larger in large ponds than they do in small ponds.

Spunky Science ™

PHOTOSYNTHESIS & CELLULAR RESPIRATION

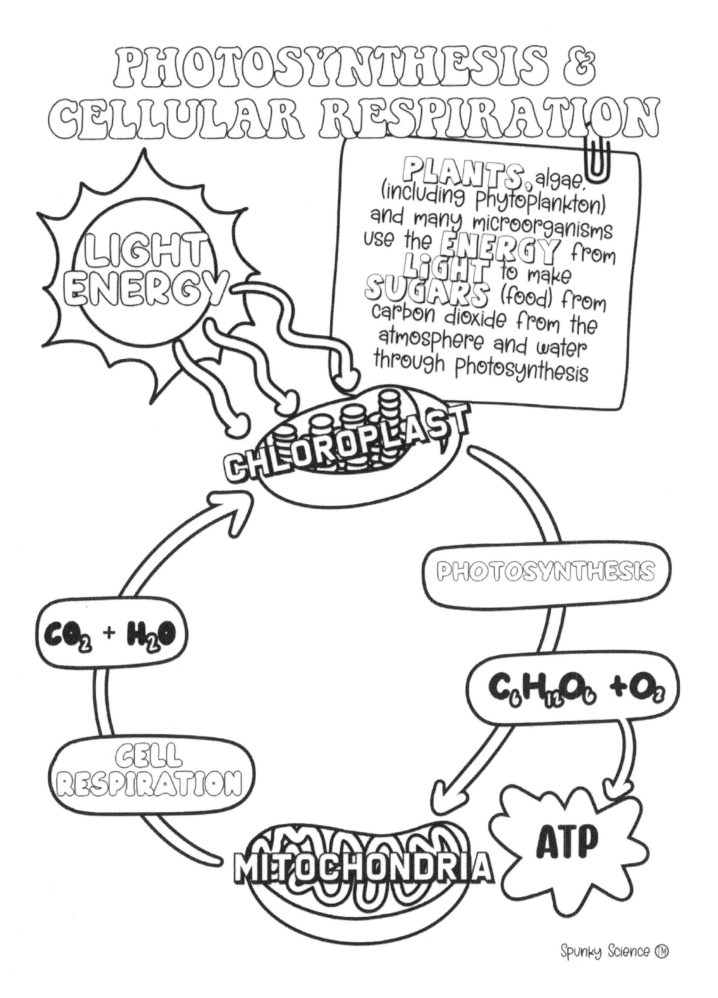

LIGHT ENERGY

PLANTS, algae, (including phytoplankton) and many microorganisms use the ENERGY from LIGHT to make SUGARS (food) from carbon dioxide from the atmosphere and water through photosynthesis

CHLOROPLAST

PHOTOSYNTHESIS

$CO_2 + H_2O$

$C_6H_{12}O_6 + O_2$

CELL RESPIRATION

MITOCHONDRIA

ATP

Spunky Science ™

CELLULAR RESPIRATION

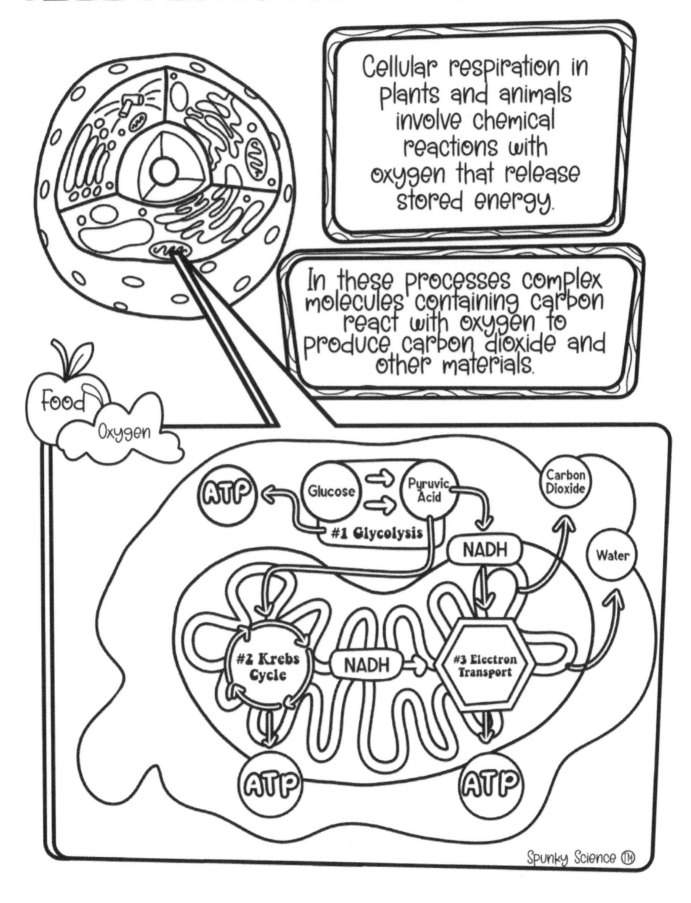

Cellular respiration in plants and animals involve chemical reactions with oxygen that release stored energy.

In these processes complex molecules containing carbon react with oxygen to produce carbon dioxide and other materials.

Food

Oxygen

ATP

Glucose

Pyruvic Acid

#1 Glycolysis

NADH

Carbon Dioxide

Water

#2 Krebs Cycle

NADH

#3 Electron Transport

ATP

ATP

Spunky Science ™

SENSORY STRUCTURES

Gathering and synthesize information that sensory receptors respond to stimuli by sending messaging to the brain for immediate behavior or storage as memories.

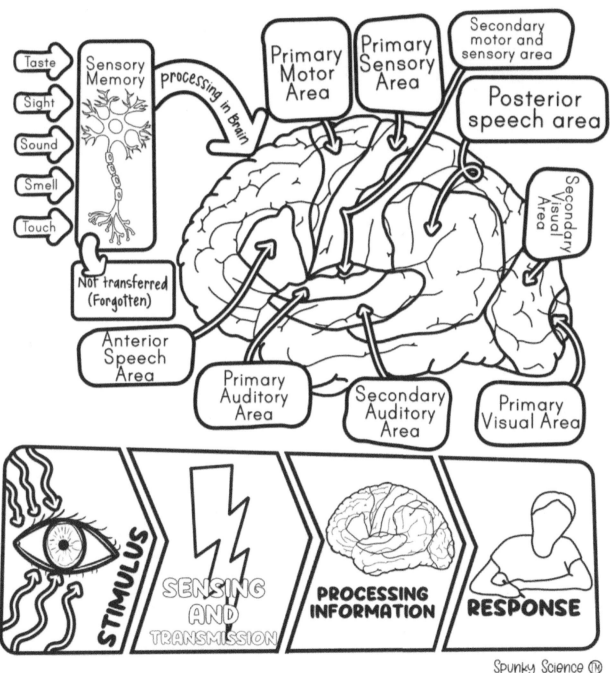

Taste

Sight

Sound

Smell

Touch

Sensory Memory

processing in Brain

Not transferred (Forgotten)

Primary Motor Area

Primary Sensory Area

Secondary motor and sensory area

Posterior speech area

Secondary Visual Area

Anterior Speech Area

Primary Auditory Area

Secondary Auditory Area

Primary Visual Area

STIMULUS

SENSING AND TRANSMISSION

PROCESSING INFORMATION

RESPONSE

Spunky Science ™

FROM MOLECULES TO ORGANISMS

```
G S B S N A G R O O R G A N E L L E S W
L I E U I U S B V S Y O I G C B B L E S
U O R R C G B R T A R I X F R R C D E H
C J A V S D L A R W I U W Y A E F E A I
O G T I A X W I E F O F S B G N E S T S
S H S V Z B E N A H G A D L P E O C V E
E F D A R E S P I R A T I O N A N B D G
O A N L V X V A C G N I D R E H A K Z A
I Y T T J S J Z F I D A R X X P F G B S
T D O P A O Y G S O Y S E S G O T T L S
S E I K H R A L U L L E C I T L U M P E
M S W O L A O T O C E L L S O I X T O M
E A Z I D E V R S E U S S I T E C U G L
T S C T X C V E X Y O Q O V D T B O S U
S V U N I C E L L U L A R N S Y N B S D
Y M O Y B I S I S E H T N Y S O T O H P
S I T C R O J N O I T C U D O R P E R O
```

- Brain
- Messages
- Herding
- Nests
- Survival
- Reproduction
- Cells
- Tissues
- Organs
- Systems
- Unicellular
- Multicellular
- Respiration
- Photosynthesis
- Oxygen
- Glucose
- ATP
- Organelles

G	S	B	N	A	G	R	O	O	R	G	A	N	E	L	E	S
H	F	U	T	R	S	B	V	S	Y	O	T	G	B	B	L	E
U	D	R	C	B	R	T	A	R	I	X	F	R	R	G	D	H
C	I	A	V	S	U	L	A	R	W	L	U	W	Y	A	E	A
I	O	T	I	A	X	W	H	E	O	F	S	R	G	N	S	T
S	H	S	V	Z	R	E	N	A	H	G	A	D	L	P	E	O
S	E	D	A	R	G	S	P	T	R	A	T	I	O	N	A	R
O	A	N	I	V	X	V	A	C	G	N	I	D	R	E	H	Z
I	L	Y	T	I	S	L	Z	Z	J	D	A	R	X	X	K	B
H	O	P	A	O	Y	G	S	G	Y	S	E	S	G	O	T	L
S	E	T	K	H	R	A	E	L	J	E	O	T	T	U	M	P
M	S	W	O	L	A	G	T	O	C	E	L	L	S	O	I	X
E	A	T	D	E	V	R	S	E	U	S	S	I	T	E	O	U
T	S	C	T	X	C	V	E	X	Y	O	O	O	V	D	T	D
S	V	U	H	I	C	E	L	L	U	L	A	R	I	N	S	Y
Y	M	O	I	R	B	I	S	I	S	E	H	T	N	Y	S	O
S	I	T	C	R	O	U	N	O	I	T	C	U	D	O	R	P

ECOSYSTEMS

ORGANIZATION IN ECOSYSTEMS

Organisms, and populations of organisms, are dependent on their environmental interactions both with other living things and non living factors

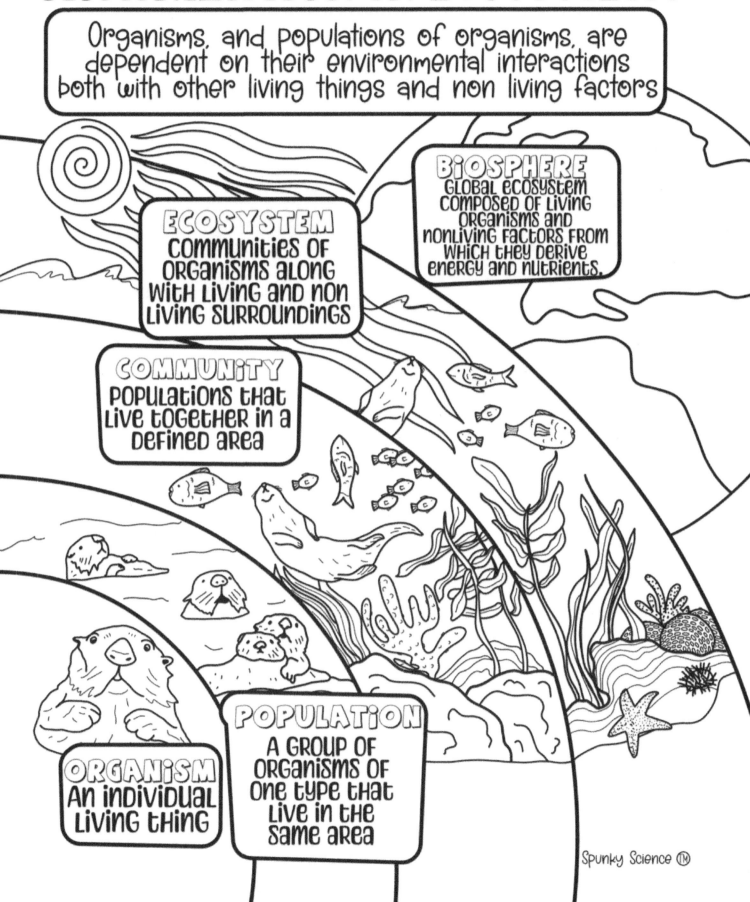

ECOSYSTEM communities of organisms along with living and non living surroundings

BIOSPHERE global ecosystem composed of living organisms and nonliving factors from which they derive energy and nutrients.

COMMUNITY populations that live together in a defined area

ORGANISM An individual living thing

POPULATION A group of organisms of one type that live in the same area

Spunky Science ™

COMPETITION FOR RESOURCES

In any ecosystem, organisms and populations with similar requirements for food, water, oxygen, or other resources may compete with other resources

Spunky Science ™

YELLOWSTONE

The wolves of Yellowstone National Park were eliminated by 1926.

Soon after, a cascade of changes altered the park's entire ecosystem.

WITH THE MAIN PREDATOR GONE...

- The Elk became overpopulated

- Mice and rabbits no longer had homes

- Pollinators had fewer flowers to feed on

- Rivers and streams became clouded with soil

- Fish struggled in murky waters

- Bears starved as they had fewer berries to feed on

- Beavers couldn't build homes without trees

- Songbirds lost their homes and food supply

Spunky Science ™

ORGANISM INTERACTIONS

PREDATORY

Predatory interactions may reduce the number of organisms or elliminate whole populations of organisms.

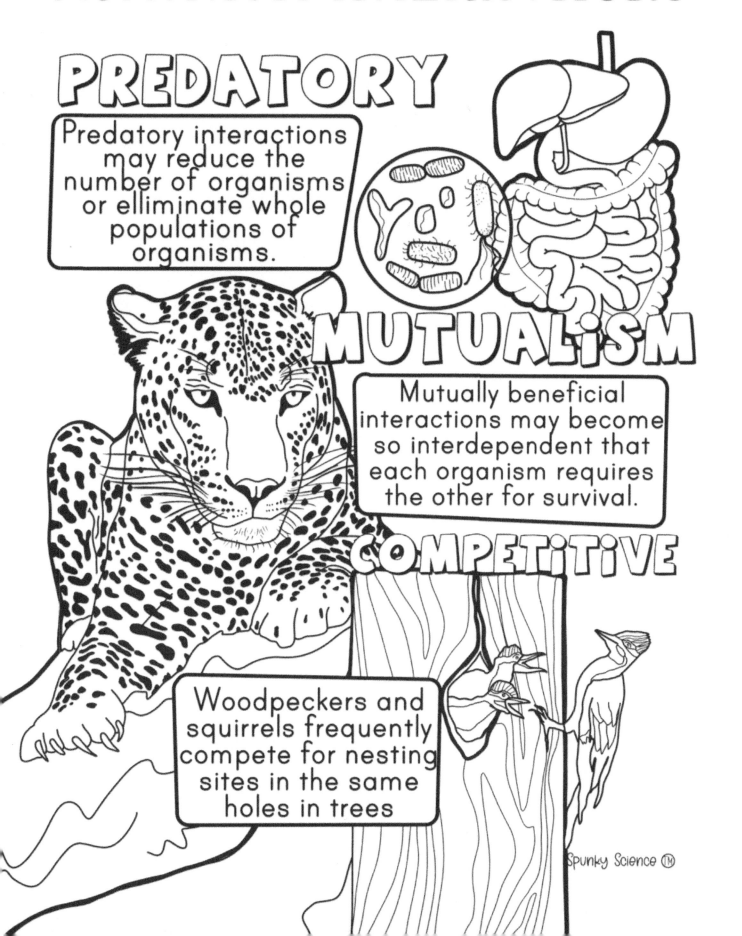

MUTUALISM

Mutually beneficial interactions may become so interdependent that each organism requires the other for survival.

COMPETITIVE

Woodpeckers and squirrels frequently compete for nesting sites in the same holes in trees

Spunky Science ™

CYCLE OF MATTER & ENERGY TRANSFER

SOIL FOOD WEB

FIRST TROPHIC LEVEL: Photosynthesis

SECOND TROPHIC LEVEL: Decomposers, mutualists, pathogens, parasites, root feeders

THIRD TROPHIC LEVEL: Shredders, predators, grazers

FOURTH TROPHIC LEVEL: Higher level predators

FIFTH+ TROPHIC LEVEL: Higher level predators

Spunky Science ™

BIODIVERSITY

Biodiversity describes the variety of species found in earths, terrestrial, and oceanic ecosystems.

Many different species of plants

One type of plant

The completeness or integrity of an ecosystems biodiversity is often used as a measure of its health.

The less diverse, the more likely this ecosystem is to be destroyed.

Spunky Science ™

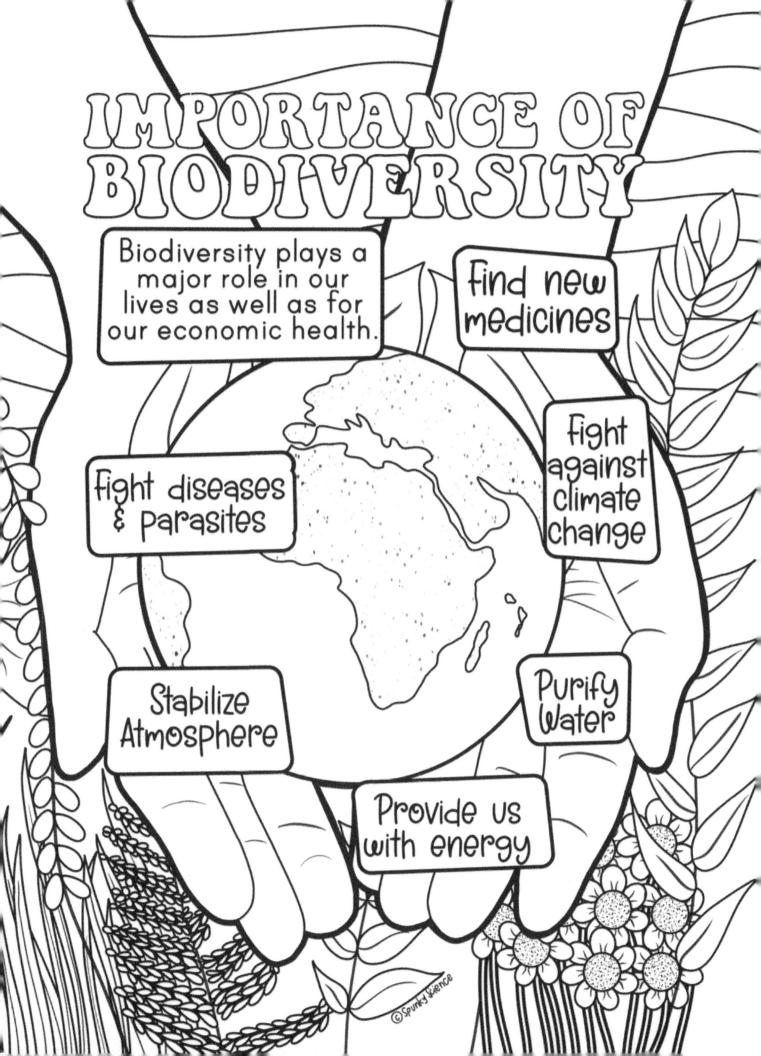

IMPORTANCE OF BIODIVERSITY

Biodiversity plays a major role in our lives as well as for our economic health

Find new medicines

Fight against climate change

Fight diseases & Parasites

Purify water

Stabilize Atmosphere

Provide us with energy

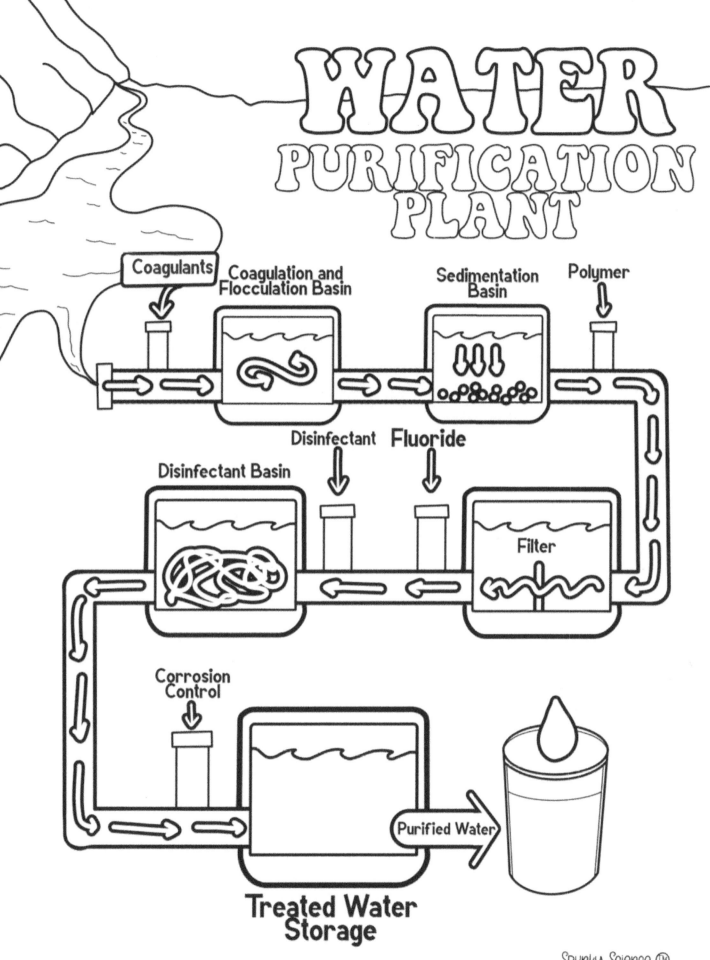

WATER PURIFICATION PLANT

Coagulants

Coagulation and Flocculation Basin

Sedimentation Basin

Polymer

Disinfectant

Fluoride

Disinfectant Basin

Filter

Corrosion Control

Purified Water

Treated Water Storage

Spunky Science ™

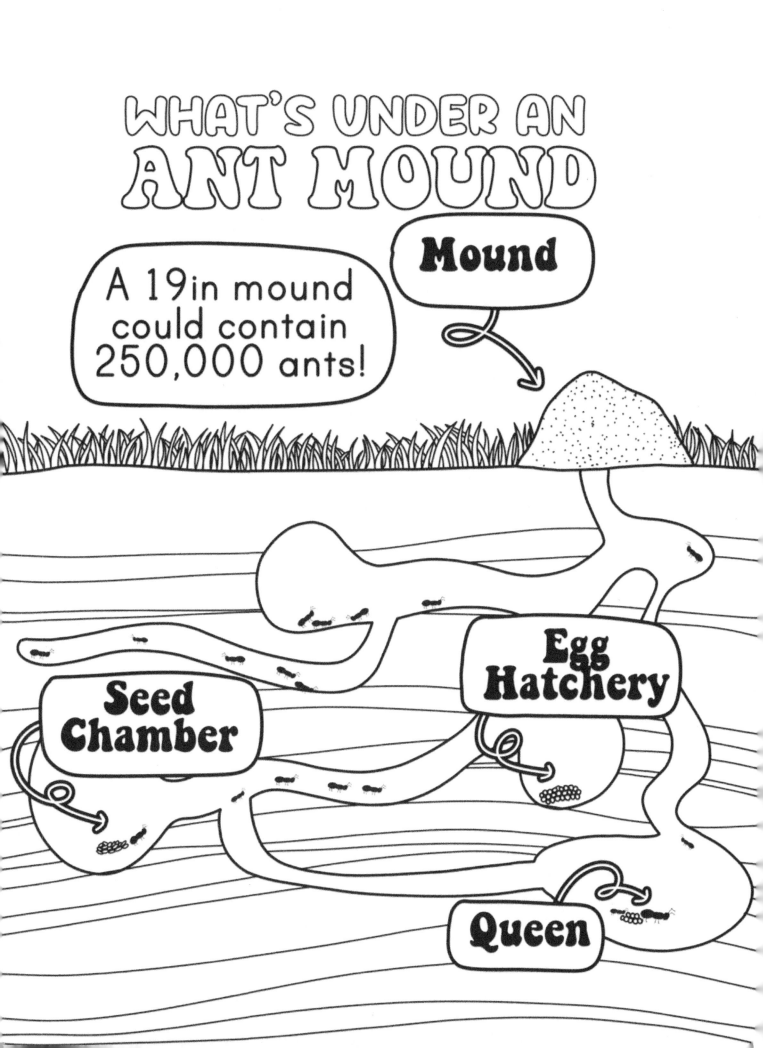

WHAT'S UNDER AN ANT MOUND

Mound

A 19in mound could contain 250,000 ants!

Egg Hatchery

Seed Chamber

Queen

ECOSYSTEMS

```
T B O E C O S Y S T E M K F C L R F L A
P I H I O S O B E E O H L D O E E Q F T
P O P U L A T I O N P K O I M A S W E F
J T F G E I X O R G A N I S M Z O D W G
D I X J N T J S I R G F D P U H U F Q D
J C Z T E D K P R S P J G V N K R V A Y
V F Q D R Z J E A E H R S F I N C V S T
J G J Z G V F R S L T K E Z T C E B F I
M H O A Y J Z E G U A T I D Y D S J G S
S I F N B Y Z S J G D N A I A H P K J R
I F D L A I B O P X K K O M P T H K N E
L S X H S C O M P E T I T I V E O M V V
A Z V F N K V T T P C F N E E O E R X I
U C F O O D Z S I H M I E L C Y C H Y D
T N J C G W S A L C L J E A K B U B I O
U K I V W E N J S A E F A S O X R F O I
M V O N P B E W D O O F I V S Z Z D V B
```

Biotic	Community	Species
Abiotic	Competitive	Resources
Ecosystem	Mutualism	Food
Population	Predatory	Energy
Biosphere	Biodiversity	Cycle
Organism	Food Web	Matter

Spunky Science ™

HEREDITY

GROWTH & DEVELOPMENT OF ORGANISMS

Organisms reproduce either sexually or asexually and transfer the genetic information to their offspring

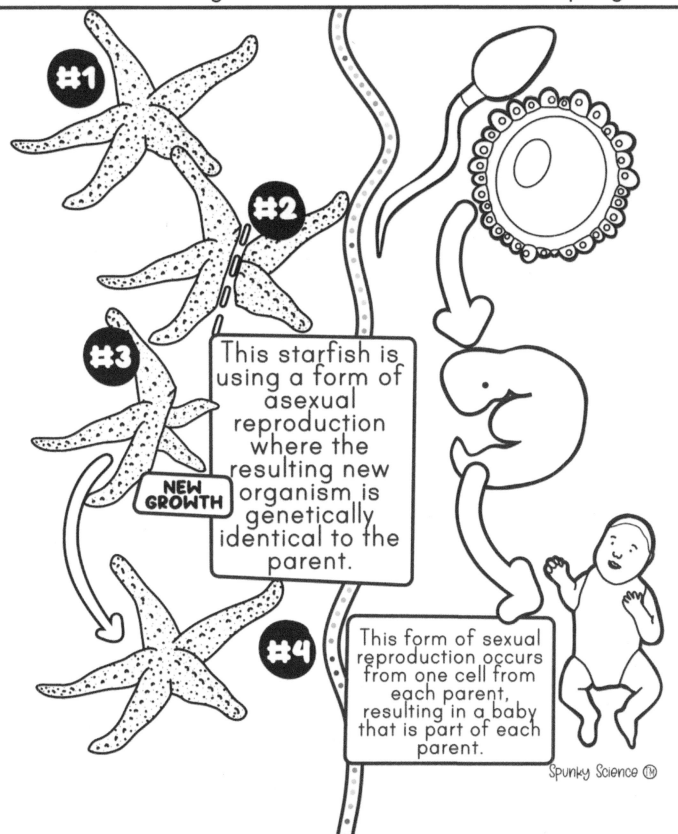

#1

#2

#3

NEW GROWTH

This starfish is using a form of asexual reproduction where the resulting new organism is genetically identical to the parent.

#4

This form of sexual reproduction occurs from one cell from each parent, resulting in a baby that is part of each parent.

Spunky Science ™

GENES

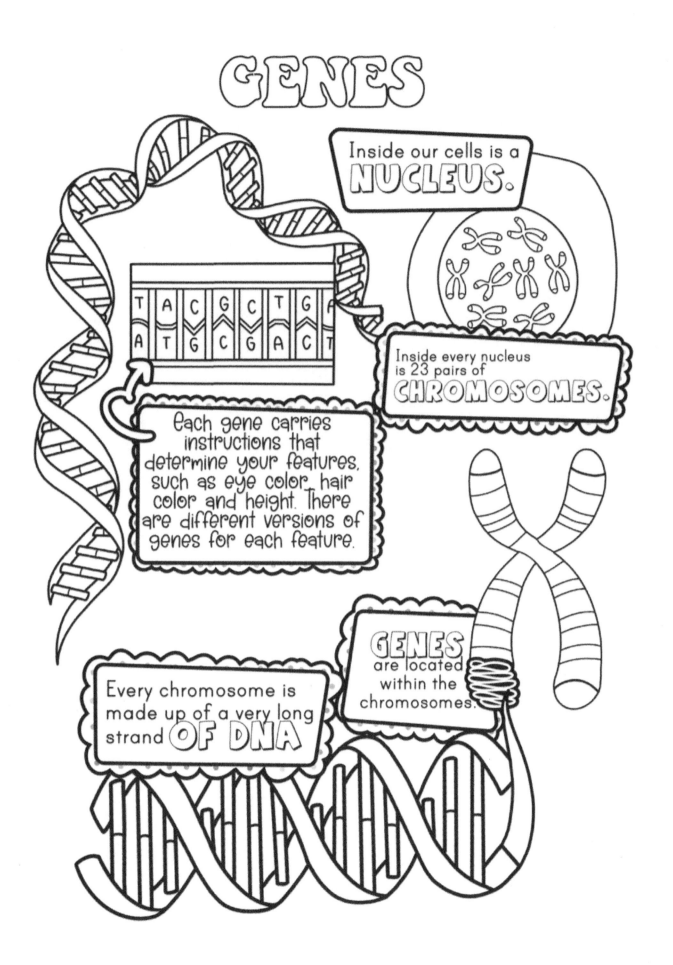

Inside our cells is a NUCLEUS.

Inside every nucleus is 23 pairs of CHROMOSOMES.

Each gene carries instructions that determine your features, such as eye color, hair color and height. There are different versions of genes for each feature.

GENES are located within the chromosomes.

Every chromosome is made up of a very long strand OF DNA

Spunky Science ™

INHERITED TRAITS

Variations of inherited traits between parent and offspring, arise from genetic differences that result from the subset chromosomes and therefore genes inherited.

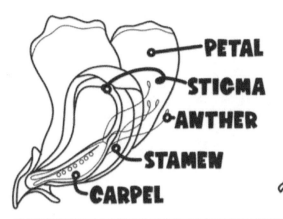

PETAL
STIGMA
ANTHER
STAMEN
CARPEL

PARENT ONE

PARENT TWO

Transferring pollen

Mendel worked with seven characteristics of pea plants: plant height, pod shape and color, seed shape and color, and flower position and color.

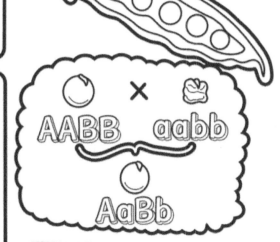

AABB × aabb

AaBb

PARENT TWO

	AB	Ab	aB	ab
AB	AABB	AABb	AaBB	AaBb
Ab	AABb	AAbb	AaBb	AAbb
aB	AaBB	AaBb	aaBB	AaBb
ab	AaBb	Aabb	aaBB	aabb

PARENT ONE

In sexually reproducing organisms, each parent contributes half of the genes aquired (at random) by the offspring. The versions can be identical or may differ from each other.

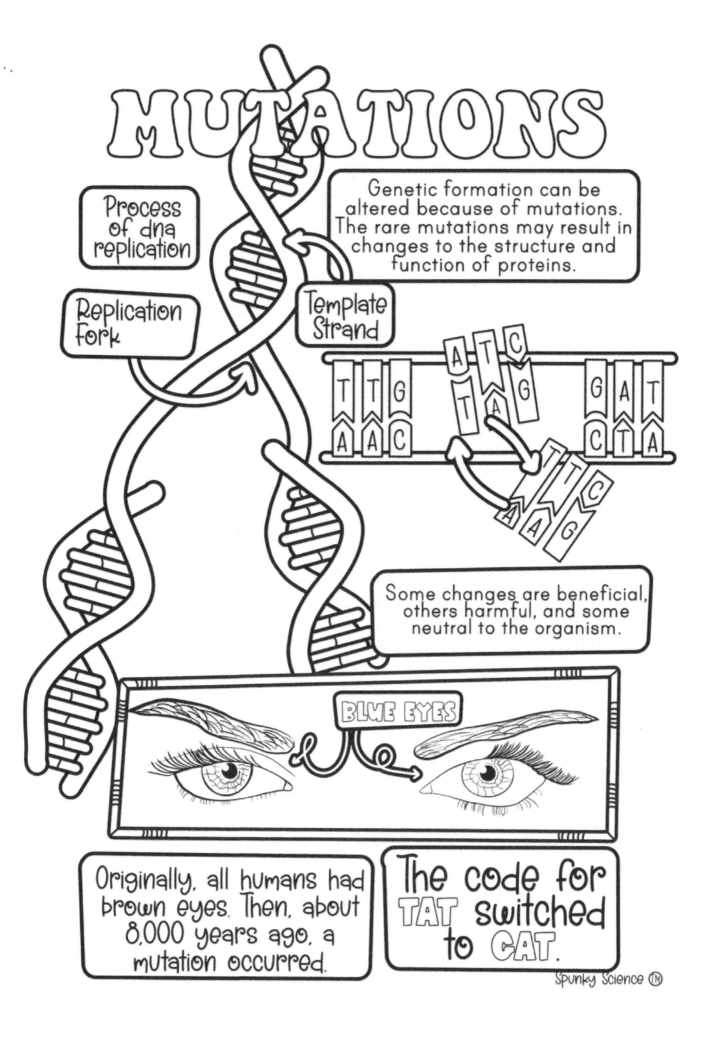

MUTATIONS

Process of dna replication

Genetic formation can be altered because of mutations. The rare mutations may result in changes to the structure and function of proteins.

Replication fork

Template Strand

Some changes are beneficial, others harmful, and some neutral to the organism.

BLUE EYES

Originally, all humans had brown eyes. Then, about 8,000 years ago, a mutation occurred.

The code for TAT switched to CAT.

Spunky Science ™

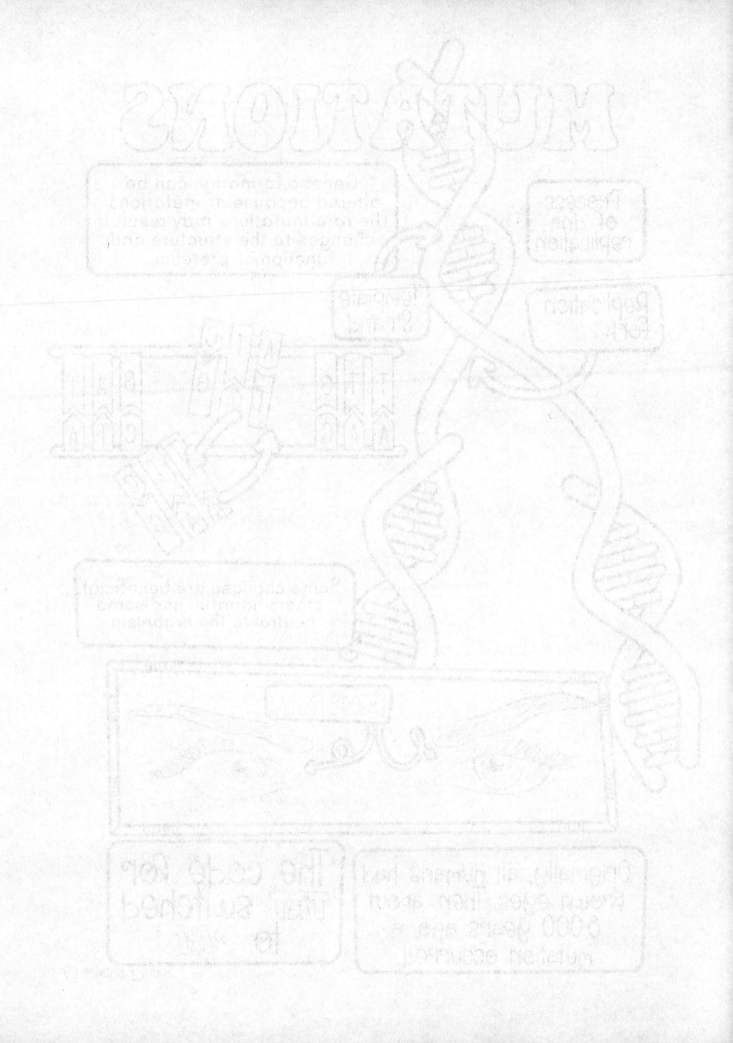

HEREDITY

```
R H M L M A H E R A U Q S T T E N N U P
O E A G N D O M I O I O R S P H A G E H
M R P D C C H R O M O S O M E A D F S Y
A E R R L I A I A Q S H G K A S R X E H
S D N E O O S O F R I O D V V J I C X G
H I B D I D Y S J F O E E F N N O H U F
K T S J E N U C L E U S T S E A O J A D
U Y A C J L S C E P N I X Z D S H J L X
F G E A C R T G T B D O S J N M R B O X
A S U F S E I N H I A J V L A U X E S A
L X N V A A A E K O O B K O I T S Q H T
L B C K P A R E N T Z N P Y B A B A U D
E O G E N E T I C S L E B E W T Q L F S
L L J O O I E A O H K R X R E I R N S C
E N V I D E N T I C A L A A H O F F X H
I C D A I L I S E O I I I S E N E G B K
S C I T S I R E T C A R A H C R O I K K
```

Sexual	Mutation	Allele
Asexual	Genes	Traits
Reproduction	Genetics	Characteristics
Heredity	Punnett Square	Parent
Mendel	Chromosome	Identical
DNA	Nucleus	Baby

Spunky Science ™

BIOLOGICAL
EVOLUTION

BIOLOGICAL EVOLUTION

GEOLOGICAL TIME

The collection of fossils in their placement in chronological order e.g. through the location of sedimentary layers in which they are found or through radioactive dating is known as fossil record. It documents the existence diversity extinction in the change of life forms throughout the history of life on earth.

Million years ago

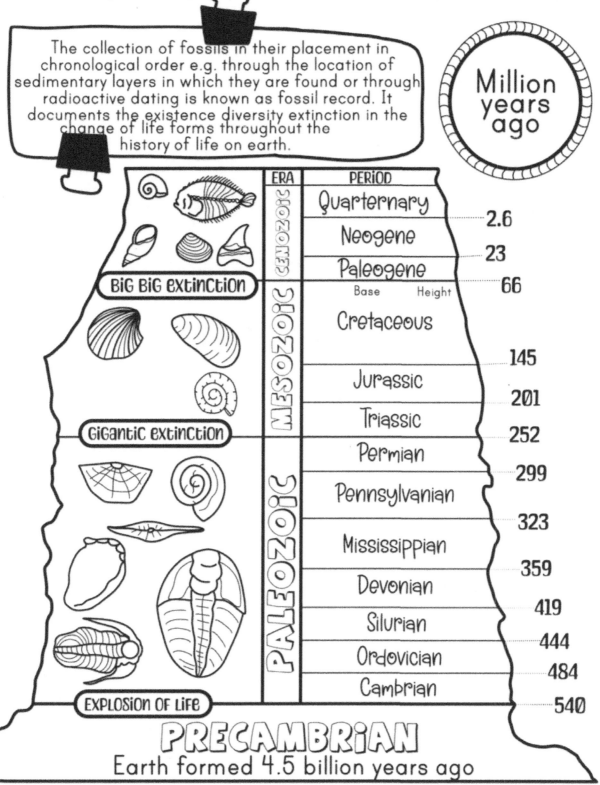

ERA	PERIOD	Million years ago
CENOZOIC	Quarternary	
	Neogene	2.6
	Paleogene	23
		66
MESOZOIC	Cretaceous (Base Height)	
	Jurassic	145
	Triassic	201
		252
PALEOZOIC	Permian	
		299
	Pennsylvanian	
		323
	Mississippian	
		359
	Devonian	
		419
	Silurian	444
	Ordovician	484
	Cambrian	540

BiG BiG extinction

GiGantic extinction

EXPLOSION OF LIFE

PRECAMBRiAN
Earth formed 4.5 billion years ago

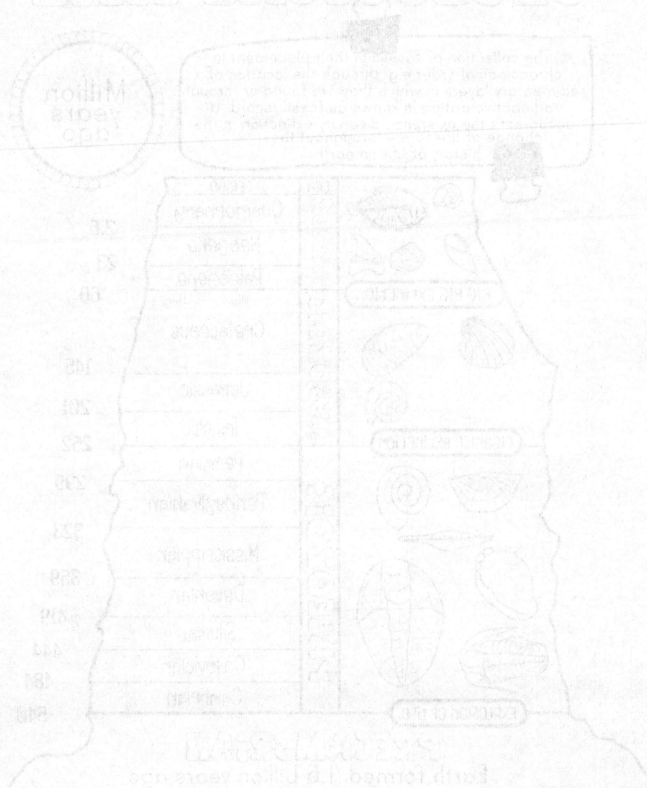

EMBRYOLOGICAL DEVELOPMENT

Comparison of the embryological development of different species reveals similarities that show relationships not evident in the fully formed anatomy.

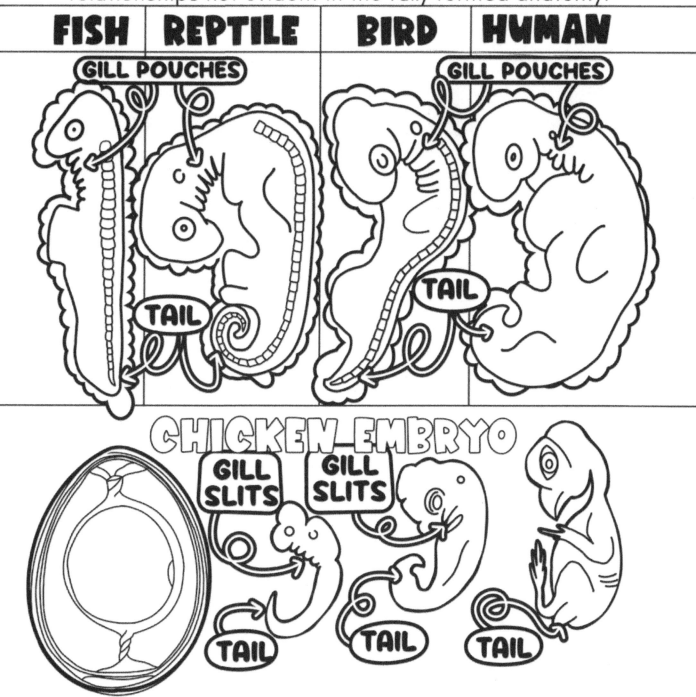

FISH	REPTILE	BIRD	HUMAN

HOMOLOGOUS STRUCTURES

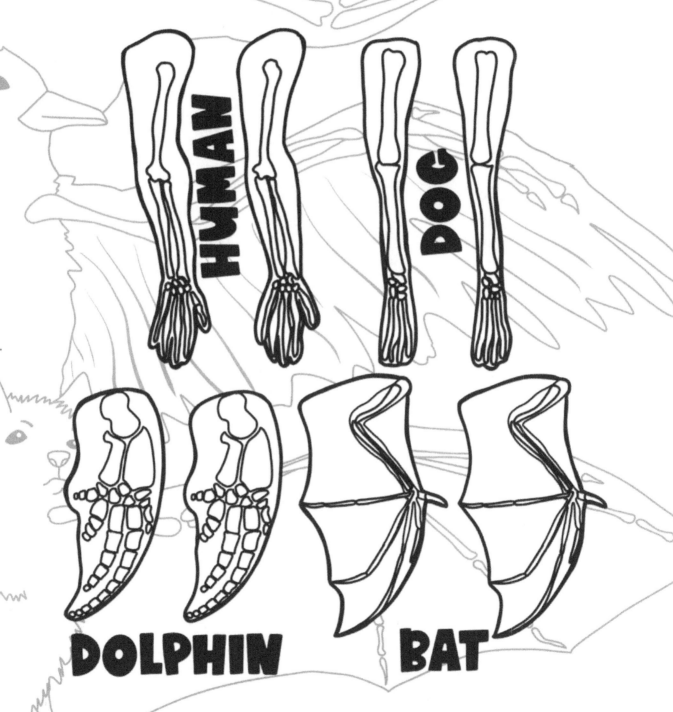

HUMAN

DOG

DOLPHIN

BAT

NATURAL SELECTION

Natural selection leads to the predominance of certain inheritance traits in a population and the suppression of others.

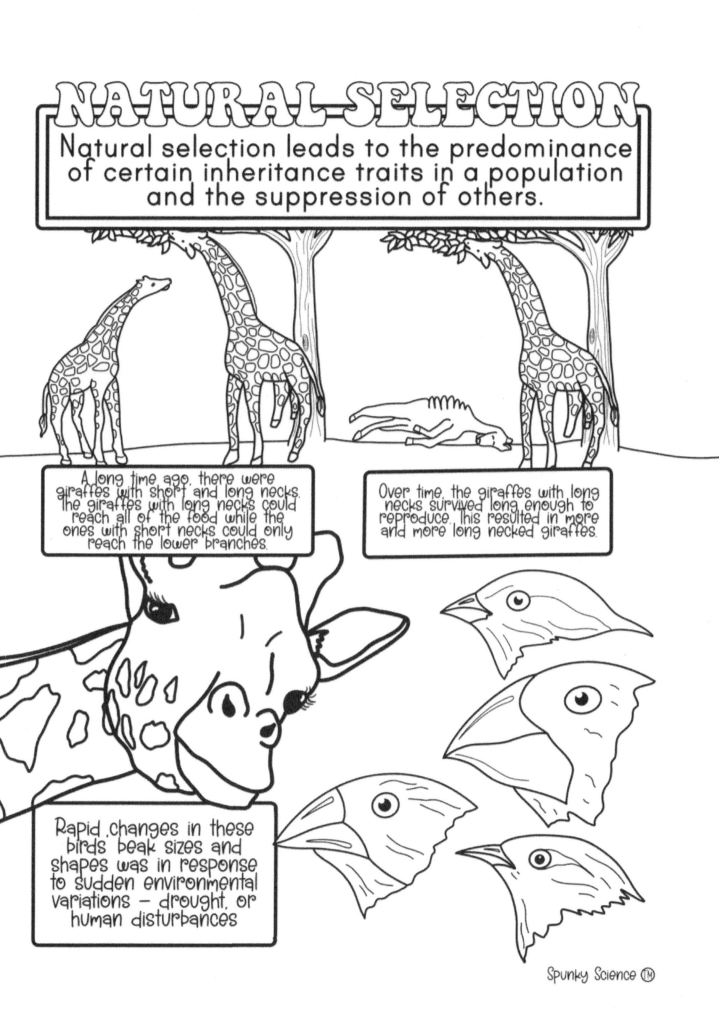

A long time ago, there were giraffes with short and long necks. The giraffes with long necks could reach all of the food while the ones with short necks could only reach the lower branches.

Over time, the giraffes with long necks survived long enough to reproduce. This resulted in more and more long necked giraffes.

Rapid changes in these birds' beak sizes and shapes was in response to sudden environmental variations — drought, or human disturbances

Spunky Science ™

ARTIFICIAL SELECTION

In artificial selection, humans have the capacity to influence certain characteristics of organisms by selective breeding. One can choose desired parental traits, determined by genes, which are then passed on to offspring.

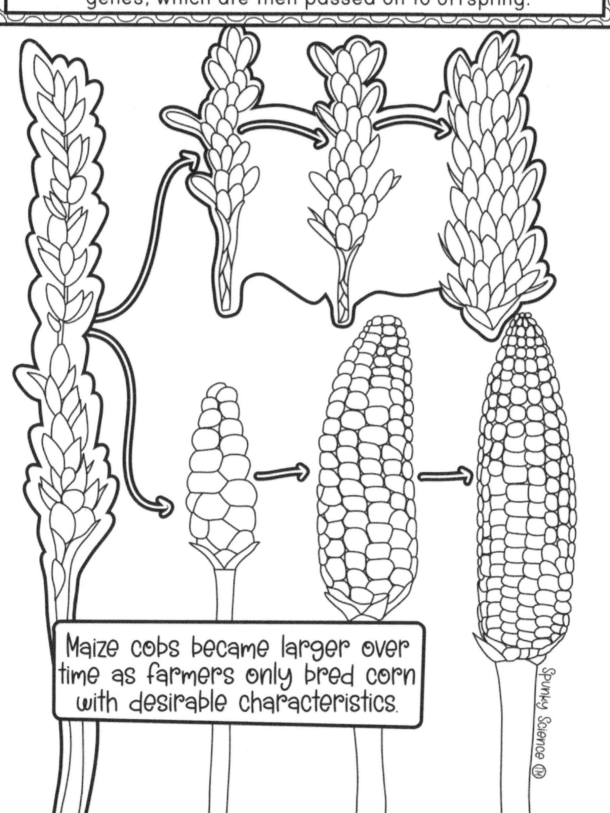

Maize cobs became larger over time as farmers only bred corn with desirable characteristics.

Spunky Science ™

ADAPTATIONS

What is that? A change or process of change by which an organism becomes better suited to fit its environment.

Discovered by... Two French scientists, named Charles Darwin and Alfred Wallace, developed a theory that states that organisms have traits that are passed down that allow organisms to survive in their environments.

Can be BEHAVIORAL OR ANATOMICAL

The way a plant or animal acts

How the plant or animal is structured

Such as

GIRAFFES with long necks are tall enough to eat and are more likely to survive.

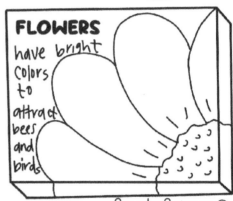

FLOWERS have bright colors to attract bees and birds

Spunky Science ©

Fur keeps BEARS warm.

PUFFER FISH take in water to look big and scare predators away

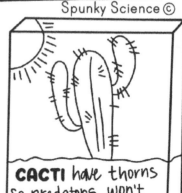

CACTI have thorns so predators won't want to eat them.

ADAPTATIONS

What is that?

A change or process of change by which an organism becomes better suited to fit its environment.

Two French scientists, named Charles Darwin and Alfred Wallace developed a theory that stated that organisms have traits that allow organisms to survive in their environment.

BEHAVIORAL OR ANATOMICAL

BIOLOGICAL EVOLUTION

```
S W A D A P T A T I O N J H L X B F G E
J Y G N I O E E R B G E B J G L I I J M
C H R F D F K M N S E L E C T I O N O B
C E Z U E A J P K G O G H J C S L L P R
L V B L C R A I A L L D A E Z S O P R Y
A P L P J T S D F T O Z V A A O G U E O
C L P O L I U A F S G N I V L F I G A L
I U I G P F V R B A I M O K H B C C C O
G T T A U I W N E C C L R L G G J A A G
O I X C G C E L K S A A A P X D L Q I I
L O N N V I D I P O L R L U B P Y A T C
O N V V Z A P R C P T U G T M V E X I A
N S S I A L L A N J S T D D M Z S H M L
O A S P E C I E S Y R A T N E M I D E S
R T F X B M F I H E N N B C F E V H Y G
H O M O L O G O U S O O K E J R W U T J
C B H G Y S C I T S I R E T C A R A H C
```

Geological	Natural	Biological
Time	Artificial	Evolution
Sedimentary	Selection	Breeding
Chronological	Behavioral	Characteristics
Homologous	Adaptation	Fossil
Structures	Embryological	Species

ANSWER KEYS!

FROM MOLECULES TO ORGANISMS

```
G S B S N A G R O O R G A N E L L E S W
L I E U I U S B V S Y O I G C B B L E S
U O R R C G B R T A R I X F R R C D E H
C J A V S D L A R W I U W Y A E F E A I
O G T I A X W I E F O F S B G N E S T S
S H S A Z B E N A H G A D L P E O C V E
E E O D A R E S P I R A T I O N A N B D
O A N L V X V A C G N I D R E H A K Z G
I Y T T J S J Z F I D A R X X P F G B A
T D O P A O Y G S O Y S E S G O T T L S
S E I K H R A L U L L E C I T L U M P S
M S W O L A O T O C E L L S O I X T O E
E A Z I D E V R S E U S S I T E C U G L
T S C T X C V E X Y O Q O V D T B O S U
S V U N I C E L L U L A R N S Y N B S D
Y M O Y B I S I S E H T N Y S O T O H P
S I T C R O J N O I T C U D O R P E R O
```

- Brain
- Messages
- Herding
- Nests
- Survival
- Reproduction
- Cells
- Tissues
- Organs
- Systems
- Unicellular
- Multicellular
- Respiration
- Photosynthesis
- Oxygen
- Glucose
- ATP
- Organelles

ECOSYSTEMS

```
T B O E C O S Y S T E M K F C L R F L A
P I H I O S O B E E O H E O A E A W E T
P O P U L A T I O N P K O I M A S W E F
J T F G E I X O R G A N I S M Z O D W G
D I C X J N T J S I R G F D P U H U F Q
J C Z T E D K P R S P J G V N K R V A D
V F Q D R Z J E A E H R S F I N C R V A
J G J Z G V F S L T K E Z T C E B F I S
M H I O A N J Z E G U A T I D Y S J J R
S I F N B Y Z S J G D N A I A H P K J E
I F D L A I B O P X K K O M P T H K N V
S X H S C O M P E T I T I V E O M V D I
A Z F N K V T T P C F N E E O E R X J D
U C F O O D Z S I H M I E L C Y C H Y O
T N J C G W S A L C L J E A K B U B I I
U K I V W E N J S A E F A S O X R F O B
M V O N P B E W D O O F I V S Z Z D V B
```

- Biotic
- Abiotic
- Ecosystem
- Population
- Biosphere
- Organism
- Community
- Competitive
- Mutualism
- Predatory
- Biodiversity
- Food Web
- Species
- Resources
- Food
- Energy
- Cycle
- Matter

HEREDITY

```
R H M L M A H E R A U Q S T T E N N U P
O E A G N D O M I O I O R S P H A G E H
M R P D C C H R O M O S O M E A D F S Y
A E R R L I A I A Q S H G K A S R I C H
S D N E O O S O F R I O D A R I C H G F
H K I B D I D Y S J F O E E F N N O H U
K U T S A C J L S C E P N I X Z D A O J
U F Y G E A C R T G T B D O S J N M R B
F A S U F S E I N H I A J V L A U X E S
L L X N V A A A E K O O B K O I T S Q H
E O B C K P A R E N T Z N P Y B A B A U
O G E N E T I C S L E B E W T Q L N F S
L L J O O I E A O H K R X R E I R N S C
E N V I D E N T I C A L A A H O F F X H
I C D A I L I S E O I I I S E N E G B K
S C I T S I R E T C A R A H C R O I K K
```

- Sexual
- Asexual
- Reproduction
- Heredity
- Mendel
- DNA
- Mutation
- Genes
- Genetics
- Punnett Square
- Chromosome
- Nucleus
- Allele
- Traits
- Characteristics
- Parent
- Identical
- Baby

BIOLOGICAL EVOLUTION

```
S W A D A P T A T I O N J H L X B F G E
J Y G N I O E E R B G E B J G L I I J M
C H R F D F K M N S E L E C T I O N C B
C E Z U E A J P K G O G H J C I S O F R
L V B L C R A I A L D A V A L P U G R Y
A P L P O L I U A F S G N M O K H B C E O
C I G P T V R B A I M O K H B C A C J T
I O T A U I W N E C C L A R L G B J A I
G X C G C E L K S A A P X D L Q A I M M
O N N V Z A I D I P O L T U G T M V E E
L O V Z A A P R C P T U G T M Z S H M S
O N S I A L A N J S T C A C N B C E V H
N S A T A S P E C I E S Y R A T N E M I D E S
R H F X B M F I H E N N B C F E V H Y G
H O M O L O G O U S O O K E J R W U T J
C B H G Y S C I T S I R E T C A R A H C
```

- Geological
- Time
- Sedimentary
- Chronological
- Homologous
- Structures
- Natural
- Artificial
- Selection
- Behavioral
- Adaptation
- Embryological
- Biological
- Evolution
- Breeding
- Characteristics
- Fossil
- Species

Made in the USA
Las Vegas, NV
01 December 2024

13058275R00046